Starting Guitar

The number one method for young guitarists

by Matt Scharfglass

WISE PUBLICATIONS
part of The Music Sales Group
London / New York / Paris / Sydney / Copenhagen / Berlin / Madrid / Tokyo

Acknowledgements

Without the help of the following people, this book never would have been possible.

Thanks go to:

Ed Lozano, Peter Pickow, and Dan Earley for their continued faith, support, and advice.

Jimmy Brown at Guitar World for his encouragement.

Sandra Keel-Huff for her fine voice-over.

Jacquelyn Marks and Astrid Naess at the East Chelsea Children's Workshop for their support and the opportunity to work with kids.

Sandy Berger for putting up with my erratic schedule.

Pete Scharfglass for his continued support and computer tips.

John Scharfglass for his insights as a teacher of guitar to children, for shuttling my equipment back and forth between Long Island and NYC, and for not taking it too hard when his name was inadvertently omitted from the acknowledgements of my last book.

Marty & Lois Scharfglass for kvelling, and for forcing those early piano lessons on me and (almost) never telling me to turn it down when I got that old, beat-up, first guitar.

And to my wife, Sandra Dubrov, for her understanding and support of this crazed musician-type who always seems to be glued to a computer, guitar, or recording console (or sometimes all three at once). And for her excellent mashed potatoes, too.

Published by

Wise Publications

14-15 Berners Street, London, W1T 3LJ, UK

Exclusive Distributors:

Music Sales Limited

Distribution Centre, Newmarket Road, Bury St Edmunds, Suffolk IP33 3YB, England.

Music Sales Corporation

257 Park Avenue South, New York, NY10010, United States of America.

Music Sales Pty Limited

120 Rothschild Avenue, Rosebery, NSW 2018, Australia.

Order No. AM945296

ISBN 0-7119-6750-4

This book © Copyright 2005 by Amsco Publications

Cover designed by Fresh Lemon

Layout by Kathy Gammon

Hand model: Cathryn Hopkins

Models: Oliver Heywood and Emma Peat, and Ruby, Jack, Lotte, Oisin, Biba, Zoe, Eve, Ryan, Amy, and Sebastian from the Crouch End Crickets.

Photography by George Taylor

Printed in China

Your Guarantee of Quality

As publishers, we strive to produce every book to the highest commercial standards.

The music has been freshly engraved and the book has been carefully designed to minimize awkward page turns and to make playing from it a real pleasure.

Particular care has been given to specifying acid-free, neutral-sized paper made from pulps which have not been elemental chlorine bleached. This pulp is from farmed sustainable forests and was produced with special regard for the environment.

Throughout, the printing and binding have been planned to ensure a sturdy, attractive publication which should give years of enjoyment.

If your copy fails to meet our high standards, please inform us and we will gladly replace it.

www.musicsales.com

Contents

Note to parents and teachers

Note to parents

When I was approached with the challenging but rewarding task of writing a guitar method for children, the first thing I did was to take a trip back to when I was around the age of the children I wrote this book for. I was about six or so, and was venturing into the world of music via piano lessons. I vividly recall about a month of summer mornings spent practicing "Hot Cross Buns" and "Row, Row, Row Your Boat" *ad nauseum* as the other six-year-olds on my block joyfully played baseball, caused bicycle crashes or otherwise got into trouble. Anyway, that was the moment where I decided that if I had to spend my summer in front of the piano, I wanted to play what I liked instead of the "baby music" that was being forced on me (remember, I was a sophisticated, worldly six-year-old). Inevitably that summer, piano lessons gave way to childhood cuts and bruises, although I decided two years later that making music was more fun than breaking my arm.

Keeping in mind that first unsuccessful flirtation with music, and the fact that kids today are more savvy than ever, I have endeavored to make the musical examples and exercises as interesting and challenging as possible. Even simple melodies such as "Twinkle, Twinkle, Little Star" have been arranged so as to keep your child from saying, "been there, done that." Most of the examples have rock-and-roll style backing tracks for the same reason.

The learning method of this book is designed so that your child, with the help of his or her teacher, can *listen* to a lesson on the accompanying CD to hear how it's supposed to sound, *practise* the lesson from the book, and then *play* along with the accompaniment.

Each track on the CD, from the "Open-string studies" through to the "Chord studies" section, has a duplicate track immediately following with the guitar part removed so that your child can play along and hear his or her progress. Some of the examples are also arranged in duet fashion so that your child can play along with a teacher or even learn both parts. The "More cool stuff to play" section contains six pieces arranged in this fashion; the CD tracks for these exercises are followed by two versions: one with the rhythm guitar part omitted, and one with the melody guitar part omitted so as to allow your child the chance to practise both parts.

Finally, prepare yourself for sore fingers. Building calluses on the fingertips is a natural and necessary side effect of playing guitar, or any stringed instrument for that matter. Reassure your child that peeling skin is no fun but in no time at all their fingers will heal (as long as they keep practising). Let them know that if their fingers hurt, it only means that their playing is getting better.

Note to the teacher

Consideration has been given in the writing of this book to the fact that most children (younger ones especially) will not be able to comfortably make a "four-fret stretch," such as a fourth-fret F♯ on the D string played with the pinky going straight into a first-fret G♯ on the G string played with the index finger. In fact, it is difficult for a child to use the fourth finger altogether. Hey, I'm an *adult* and *my* pinky barely works. So, in keeping with this and the fact that this is a beginner's book, almost all of the musical examples herein are written within a three-fret span, concentrating on the first, second, and third fingers.

About your child's instrument

The quality of the guitar is an important aspect in the learning process; a bad-sounding, difficult-to-play guitar that barely stays in tune will not do justice to your child's hard work, and will most likely lead to frustration as your child will wonder why he or she is practising so much but not sounding any better. While the reluctance to spend a lot of money on something that may not work out is definitely something I can relate to (I'm a musician!), keep in mind that the amount of aggravation, time, and money spent on repairs and adjustments saved in the long run will more than justify the expense of a decent instrument that your child won't outgrow too quickly. Don't worry, it doesn't have to be £2000 (or even £200) and custom-made from exotic woods from the Brazilian rainforests.

If you are currently shopping for a guitar for your child, stay away from the so-called "student models." Get a regular, low-end (in terms of cost) instrument; most of the major guitar manufacturers produce a line of decent instruments in the under-£200 range. If you can find one that's small-scale or half-sized, so much the better. The *action*, or distance of the strings from the fingerboard, should be as low as possible, but high enough so that the strings don't buzz against the frets.

There are two main types of acoustic guitars: steel-string and nylon-string. Both have boons and benefits; I'll briefly explain them. Steel-string guitars are generally louder; consequently they are mainly used for rock, folk, country, and even funk. They tend to have narrower necks, thus better enabling children to get their hands around them. Nylon-string guitars generally have a mellower tone, making them perfect for classical or Latin music. These guitars have wider necks, which will make them more difficult for children to use but will better train their hand muscles to stretch and strengthen. Aside from the type of music being played, neither is better than the other for any particular purpose. If buying from a music store, and if possible, have one of the salespeople play the prospective purchase in front of you. If they can't make it sound reasonably good, your child certainly won't be able to. Also be sure to detune the strings if the guitar isn't going to be used for a long time; wood is sensitive to weather changes and prolonged string tension may warp the neck and body.

Parts of the guitar

Before we begin playing, let's take a look at your instrument.

The headstock is the top of the guitar. The headstock holds the tuning pegs. The strings are wound around the pegs; you tune up the guitar by turning the pegs.

The little white plastic thing that comes next is called the nut.

After this is the fretboard, which is where your fingers go when you are playing. The fretboard has many thin metal strips on it; these are called frets. They show you where your fingers are supposed to go, and separate one note from the next.

The hole in the middle of the body of your guitar is called the soundhole.

Finally, down at the bottom where the strings end, is the bridge.

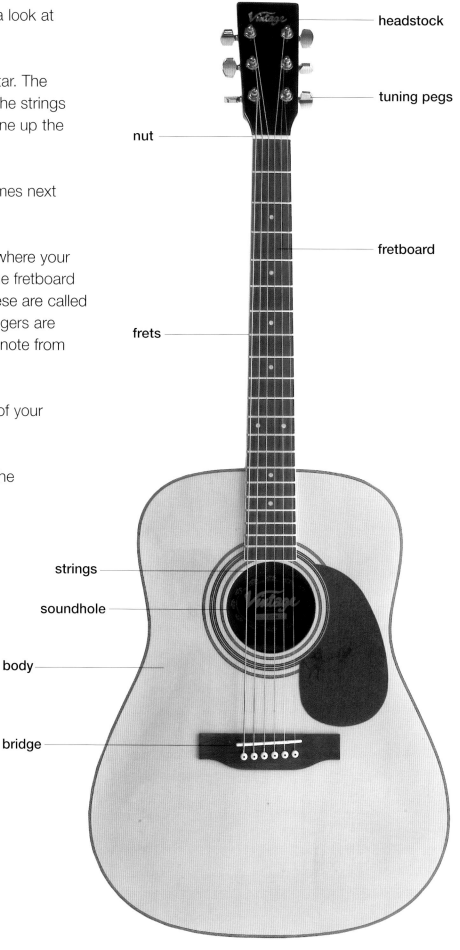

headstock

tuning pegs

nut

fretboard

frets

strings

soundhole

body

bridge

TIP

When not being played, try to keep your guitar in its case, away from heat and direct sunlight where it can't be knocked over. Avoid exposing your instrument to extremes of temperature.

Holding the guitar

You can hold your guitar either standing up or sitting down.

Standing: It's always best to use a strap when standing up with your guitar. Adjust the strap so the guitar is at a sensible height (not too high or low, just sitting comfortably over the tummy area) and position it so there is an equal balance of weight.

Sitting: Look at the picture below. Your arms should never take the whole weight of the guitar; they should be free to just play it. Rest the body of the guitar on your right knee (or left if you are playing a left-handed guitar) and put your other leg slightly out for extra support. Don't slouch!

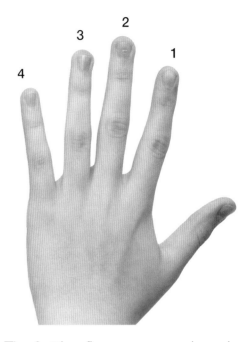

The fretting fingers are numbered 1, 2, 3, and 4. Try to keep your left hand relaxed. The left-hand thumb should be roughly vertical behind the neck and roughly behind the 1st and 2nd fingers.

Open-string studies

E A D

High E B G

There are six strings on a guitar. Each one makes a different note, and each note has its own name. The names of the strings are E, A, D, G, B, and high E.

This is what the notes look like on a music staff:

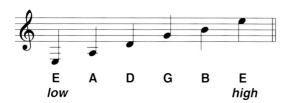

E A D G B E
low   *high*

TIP If you're not sure whether a string is in tune or not, loosen the string slightly, listen to the notes on track 1 and little by little, tighten the string until it sounds exactly the same as the note you hear on the CD.

Let's begin playing right away. We'll start with songs that use these strings. But first, we'll learn how to hold a guitar pick.

Make an "O.K." sign with your hand, like in the picture.

Then take your pick and put it between your thumb and first finger. If you have trouble, then ask your teacher or mum or dad to show you the proper way to hold a pick.

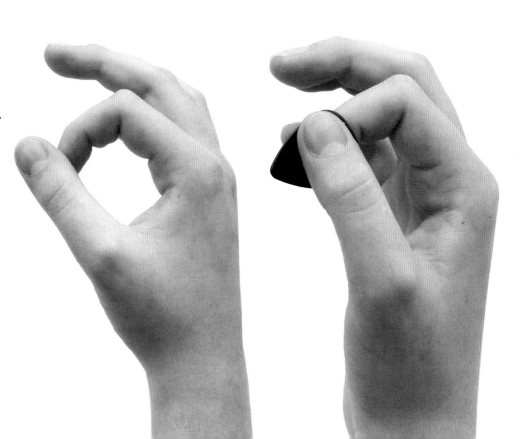

Are you holding the pick correctly? Good. Go ahead now and try plucking the strings with the pick. Your wrist should be nice and relaxed. Now that you know how to hold your pick, we can begin playing.

Listen to the songs below on the CD so you can hear what they sound like; then practise them so you can get used to playing your guitar. When you're ready, play along with the CD and have fun!

 ## Example 1

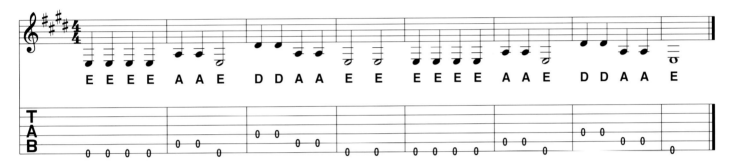

 ## Example 2

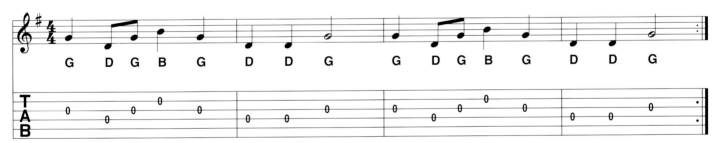

 ## Example 3

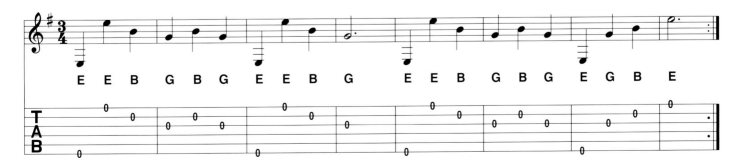

Melodic studies

Fretting notes – the high E string

Now you are ready to play other notes on the fretboard. As you already know, the fretboard has lots of thin metal strips called *frets*; these mark where the notes are. Press down hard with your first finger on the highest string (the high E string) just behind the second fret. Don't press on the fret itself or the note won't sound properly.

Don't worry if it hurts your finger a little at first. The more you practise, the more you will get used to it, and the better you will play.
Is the note ringing nice and clearly? If it's buzzing, try moving your hand back a little bit from the fret and make sure you are pressing hard on the string.

Just like notes from the open strings have their own names, fretted notes have their own names too. For example, the note you're playing now is F♯. In music, it looks like this:

Let's learn more notes on the two high strings: high E and B.

The note on the fourth fret of the high E string is G♯. The note on the third fret is G; and you already know that the note on the second fret is F♯.

G♯

G

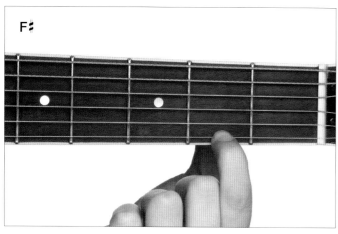

F♯

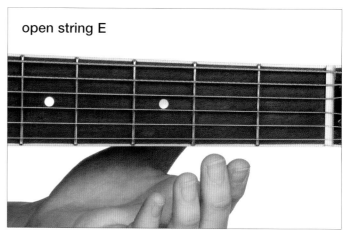

open string E

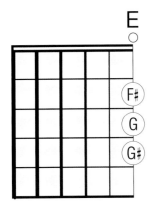

E

Location of notes
on the high E string

In written music they look like this:

G# G F# E

Fretting notes – the B string

Now let's take a look at the B string.

On the fourth fret we have D♯; the note on the third fret is D; and on the second fret, C♯.

D♯

D

C♯

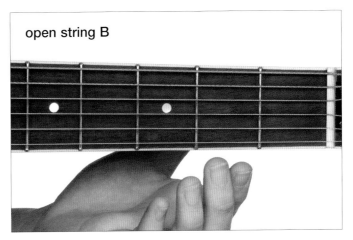

open string B

11

Melodic studies

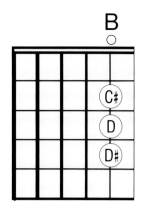

B

Location of notes on the B string

In written music they look like this:

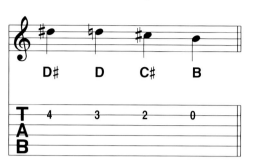

D♯   D   C♯   B

```
T  4    3    2    0
A
B
```

Take a look at the music below. The numbers above the notes tell you which fingers to play the notes with. A number *1* means to use your *index* finger. Number *2* means use your *middle* finger. Number *3* means use your *ring* finger, and a number *4* means use your *pinky*.

An "0" means to play the open string. Since the number above the first note is a 3, that means you play the first note using your ring finger. The letters below the notes tell you what the notes are in case you forget. Are you ready to try your first song using fretted notes?

9 & 10

Example 4: Pachelbel's Canon

play four times

3   1   0   3   1   0   1   3   3

G♯   F♯   E   D♯   C♯   B   C♯   D♯   G♯

Did all the notes sound clear? Did any of them buzz? If you had any trouble, just go back and try again. Play each note slowly until you can get it to sound good. Let's try one more song before we move on.

11 & 12

Example 5

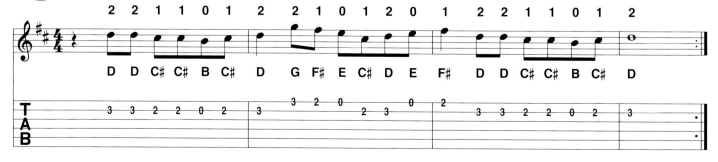

2 2 1 1 0 1 2   2 1 0 1 2 0 1   2 2 1 1 0 1 2

D D C♯ C♯ B C♯ D   G F♯ E C♯ D E F♯   D D C♯ C♯ B C♯ D

Fretting notes – the G string

Now let's move on to the two middle strings, G and D.

The note on the fourth fret of the G string is B; on the third fret we have B♭; and the note on the second fret is A.

B

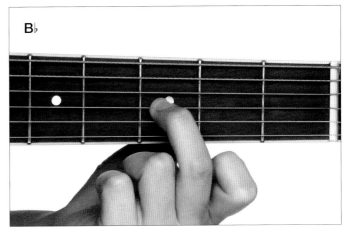

B♭

A

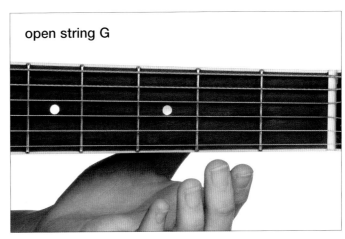

open string G

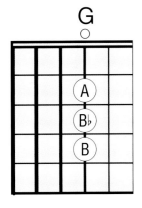

G

Location of notes
on the G string

This is how they look in written music:

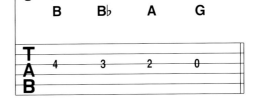

B   B♭   A   G

Melodic studies

Fretting notes – the D string

The note on the fourth fret of the D string is F♯; on the third fret we have F; and on the second fret, E.

Practice these notes until you are comfortable with them. Remember to look at the numbers above the notes so you know which fingers to use. When you are ready, we'll play a few more songs.

F♯

F

E

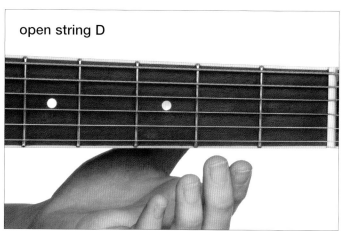

open string D

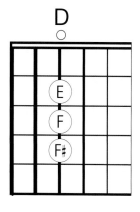

D

Location of notes on the D string

In written music they look like this:

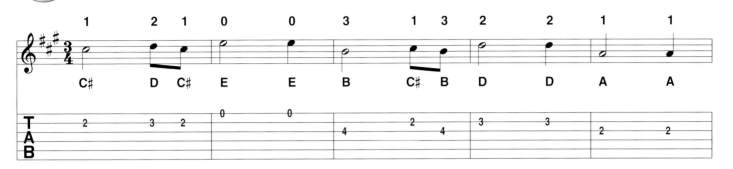

14 & 15 Example 6: Sonata in A

W.A. Mozart

16 & 17 Example 7

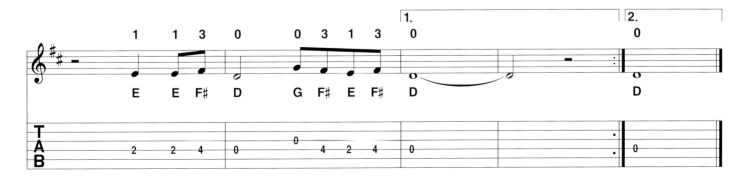

Melodic studies

18 & 19 **Example 8: O Sacred Head**   J.S. Bach

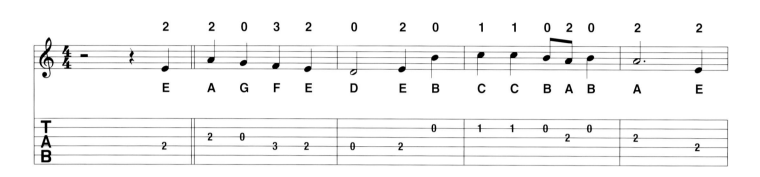

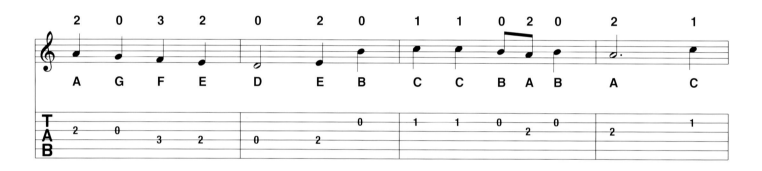

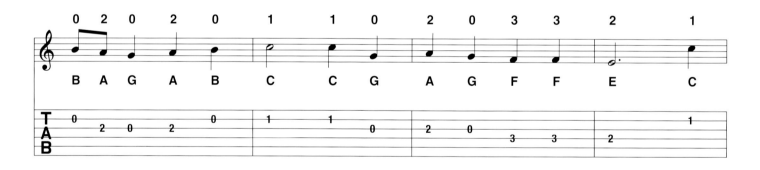

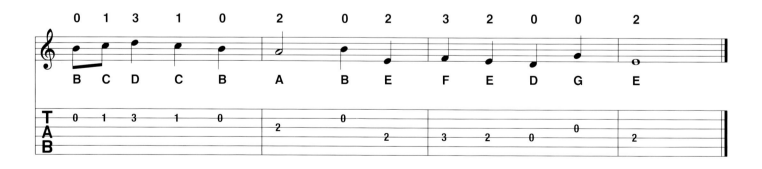

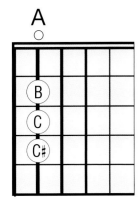

Fretting notes – the A string

Finally, let's learn what notes we can find on the two low strings, A and E.

The note on the fourth fret of the A string is C♯; the third fret is C; and on the second fret we have B.

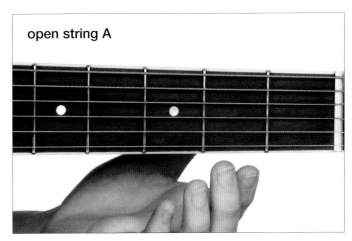

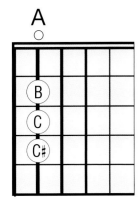

Location of notes on the A string

In written music they look like this:

Melodic studies

Fretting notes – the low E string

The notes on the low E string are the same as those on the high E string… remember what they are?

G♯

G

F♯

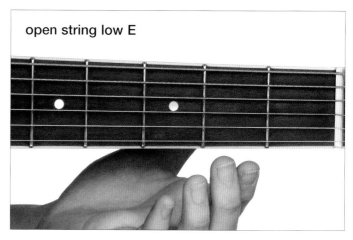

open string low E

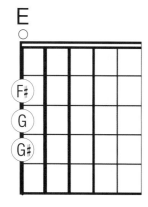

E

Location of notes on the low E string

In written music they look like this:

18

Even though the notes on the low E string sound different from the notes on the high E string, the names of the notes are the same.

This is because the notes have the same pitch, but they sound different because they're in different *octaves*. For example, let's try "Mary Had A Little Lamb" on the *low* E string.

(Low) Mary Had A Little Lamb

Now let's try it on the *high* E string.

(High) Mary Had A Little Lamb

Can you hear the difference? (High) "Mary Had A Little Lamb" is in a different octave than (Low) "Mary Had A Little Lamb," but they both sound alike.

Now that you know what notes are on all six strings, let's finish this part of the book by playing some songs which contain the notes we've learned. If you're having trouble with any of these songs, practise each note slowly until you can play the song easily.

Melodic studies

 23 & 24 Example 9

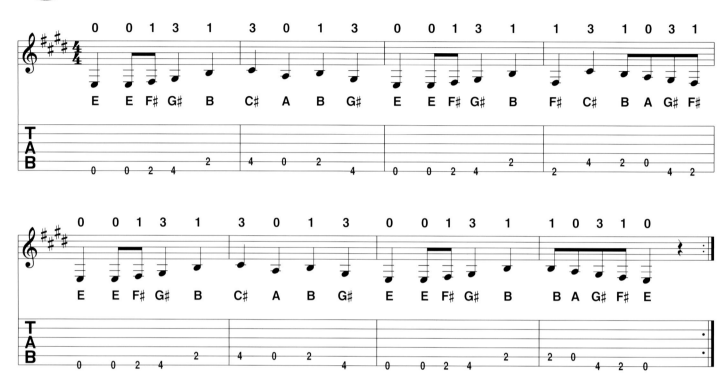

Here's one you already know...

25 & 26 Example 10: Twinkle, Twinkle Little Star

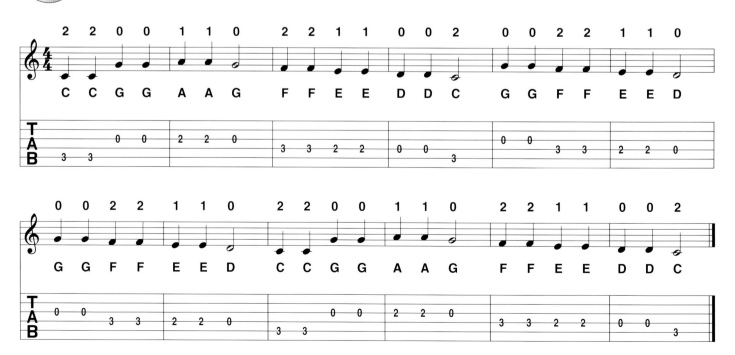

Example 11: G Blues Bassline

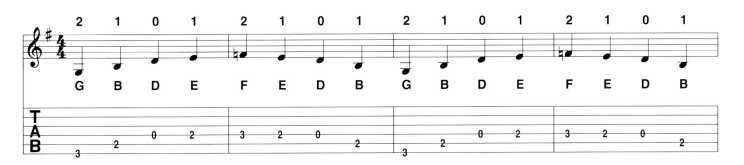

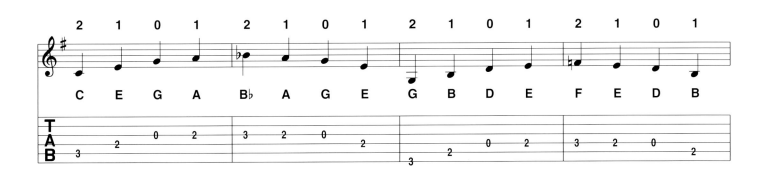

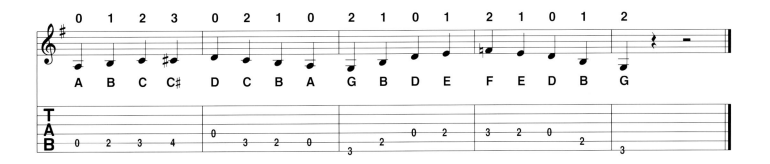

CHECKPOINT
WHAT YOU'VE ACHIEVED SO FAR

You can now:
- Name each part of the guitar
- Hold your guitar properly

- Tune your guitar
- Hold your pick properly
- Fret notes on all strings

Now turn the page for the last piece in this section – "Danny Boy." This is longer than the others and makes a great concert piece!

Melodic studies

29 & 30 **Example 12: Danny Boy**

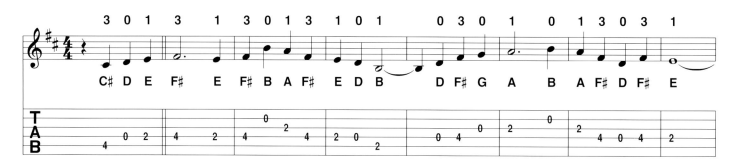

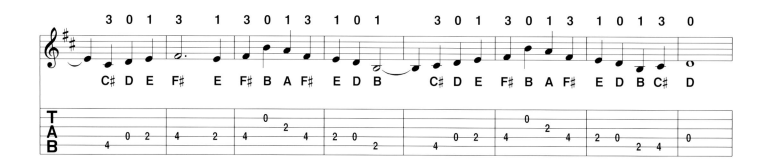

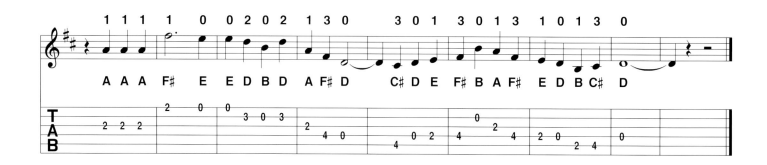

Congratulations... you now know how to play melodies and songs on the guitar!

Chord studies

 31 A chord is a bunch of notes that sound good when played together. Chords are used to accompany melodies like the ones you've just learned how to play.

One-finger chords

Key of C

All you need is one finger to play a chord. It's that easy. Do you have a finger? Great! Let's get started.

The first chord we're going to learn is the C chord. Look at the picture below; it shows you which strings to play, and the little circle with the number in it shows you which fret to put your finger behind. The number inside the circle shows you which finger to use. Since the number is 1, that means you should use your first finger (your index finger), and since the circle comes right before the first line in the picture, that means you put your first finger behind the first fret. Also, don't play the strings that have Xs over them.

Meanwhile, we are also going to learn how to strum with the other hand. Strumming means using your pick to play more than one string at the same time. All you have to do is hold the pick and brush down over the strings with it, toward the floor. Remember to keep your wrist nice and relaxed.

Are you ready to play? Press down hard on the string, and strum the chord a few times to get used to it. When you're comfortable with the C chord, we'll also learn the G and G7 chords since they often go with the C chord.

With the G chord, you'll need to use your third finger (your ring finger), because the circle in the picture has a 3 in it. The circle comes right before the third line in the picture, so this means you put your third finger behind the third fret.

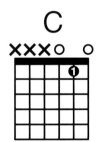

C chord

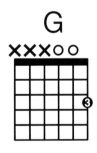

G chord

Chord studies

Look at the picture for the G7 chord. The circle has the number 1 in it, and it comes right before the first line in the picture. This means to put your first finger behind the first fret.

G7

G7 chord

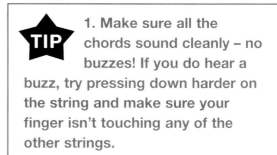

TIP

1. Make sure all the chords sound cleanly – no buzzes! If you do hear a buzz, try pressing down harder on the string and make sure your finger isn't touching any of the other strings.

2. Play in time with the chords on the beat. Don't worry about playing a continuous rhythm right away. Just get comfortable with the changes and introduce more strumming as you gain confidence.

Before we play our first song, let's practise playing all three chords smoothly. We'll play the exercise below slowly to get you used to playing one chord after another.

 ## Example 13

Is it getting easier? Good. Now you are ready to play your first song with chords.

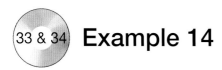 ## Example 14

35 One more chord that you need only one finger to play is *Em*. This chord also sounds good with C chords.

Look at the circle in the picture.

Which finger should you use?

Which fret does your finger go behind?

Which strings have Xs over them?

Which string should you press?

Em

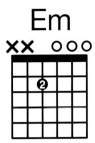

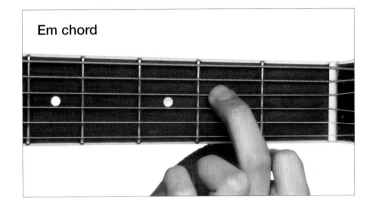

Em chord

 36 & 37 # Example 15

| C | Em | G | G7 | C | | C | C | Em | Em | G | G7 | C |

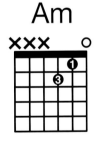 **38** ## Two-finger chords

Another chord that goes with C chords is *Am*. This chord requires two fingers, so if you have another finger, now would be a good time to use it.

Am

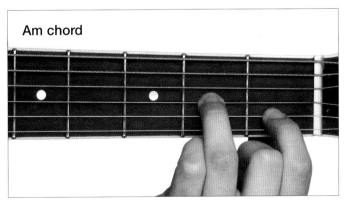

Am chord

Look at the picture to the right to see where your fingers go. Notice that there's a circle on the G string with the number 3 in it. This means you should press down on the G string with your third finger (your ring finger). Since the circle comes right before the second line, your finger goes right behind the second fret, and, of course, the circle with the 1 in it means you put your first finger behind the first fret (but you knew that already).

Practise playing the Am chord until it feels comfortable. When you can play it easily, we'll move on to our next song.

Chord studies

Before we start playing the song, let's listen to it on the CD. You might notice that it's a little faster than what you've been playing so far. In order to strum chords quickly, we use *downstrums* and *upstrums*.

A *downstrum* is when you strum a chord in a downward motion. You've been using downstrums all along up to this point, so you already know how to do it. Whenever you see this symbol, ⊓, it means you should *downstrum* the chord.

downstrum

Playing a repeated chord quickly is hard to do with just downstrums, so we use *upstrums* to make it easier. An *upstrum* is when you strum a chord in an upward motion. Whenever you see this symbol, ⋁, it means you *upstrum* the chord. Listen to the following song on the CD one more time. Then look at the music and practise downstrumming and upstrumming the chords. When you can do it easily, play along with the CD.

upstrum

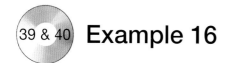

Example 16

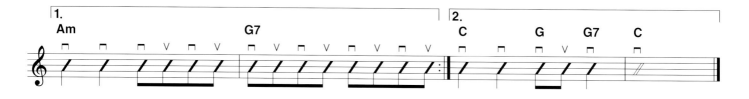

Another chord that sounds good with C chords that also uses two fingers is *F*. Here's another picture to show you how to play it.

F

Wait a minute... the picture says to put your first finger on the B string and high E string at the same time. How do we do that? It's easy: Put your first finger behind the first fret on the B string, just like it says in the picture. Then make sure your finger is flat so that you're pressing on the high E string also. There... now you are pressing on two strings with the same finger. It might hurt your finger a little bit, but don't worry, you're just not used to it yet. Keep practising and it will get much easier.

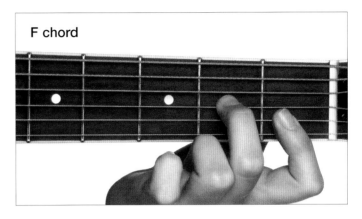

F chord

Here's a song that uses all six of the chords we've learned so far. Don't forget to use downstrums and upstrums.

Example 17

Chord studies

Three-finger chords

Now that you can play these chords, let's add more notes to them so that they sound bigger and louder. We'll begin with the C chord. Simply strum the chord, and then look at the picture below to see where the rest of your fingers go.

See the circles that have the numbers 2 and 3 in them? You guessed it... this means to press down on the A and D strings with your nose and stand on your head. Or something like that.

Sounds better, doesn't it? Now do the same with the G, G7, Em, Am and F chords.

C

C chord

G

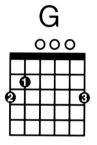

G chord

G7

G7 chord

Em

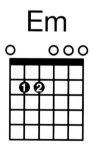

Em chord

Am

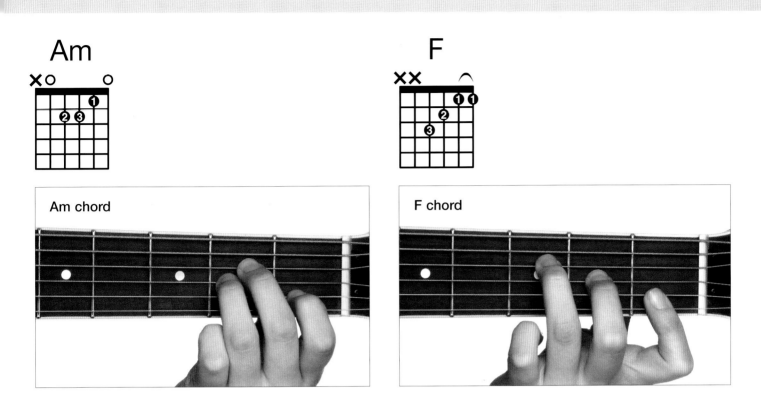

F

Am chord

F chord

Now we'll play the last song again using these new chords.

45 & 46 **Example 17**

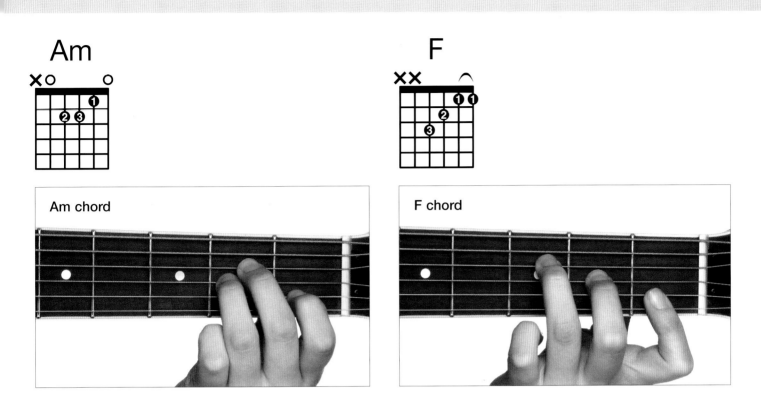

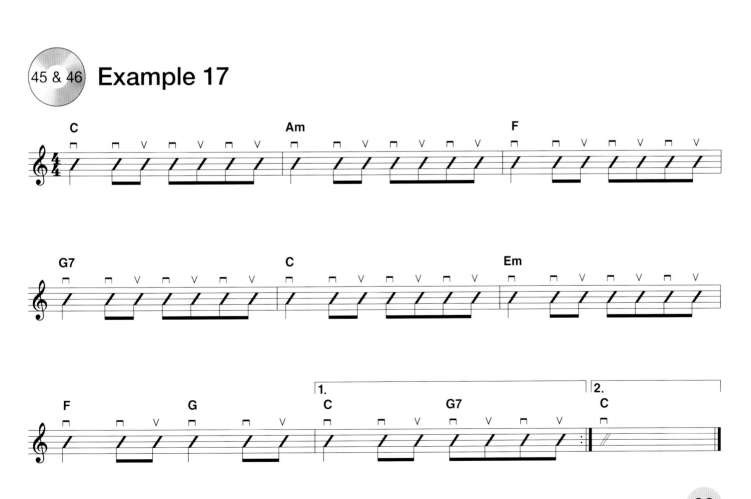

Chord studies

Key of G

Every chord has a bunch of other chords that sound good when you play them together. For example, the C chord sounds good with G, G7, Em, Am and F chords. The G chord sounds good with the C chord and the *D* chord. You already know how to play a G and a C; the picture to the right shows how to play a D.

Let's now learn a new song with our new chord. If you feel like it, why not learn the melody, too? All the melody notes are on the G and D strings.

D

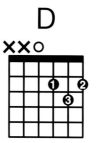

D chord

48 & 49 **Example 18**

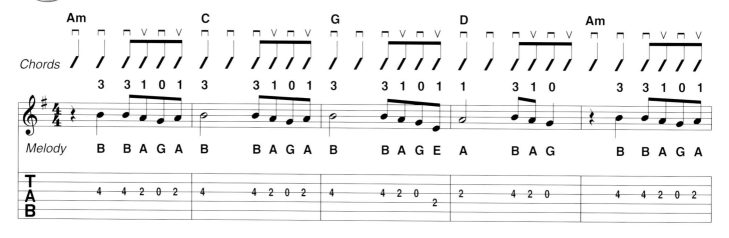

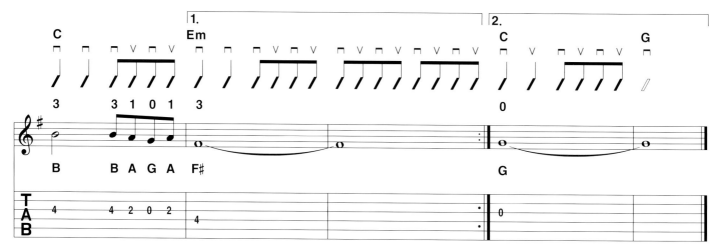

Our next song has the new D chord, plus many other chords you already know. You might want to take a minute to practise each chord slowly to make sure that you can play one after the other smoothly.

Since this one is a little slower, you can downstrum all the chords. All the melody notes are on the B and G strings.

Example 19

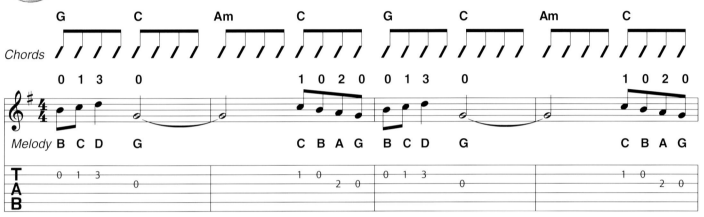

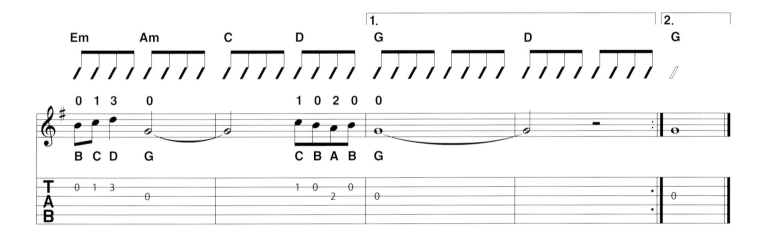

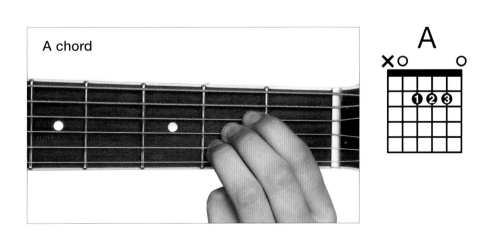

Key of D

Like G chords and C chords, the D chord also has chords that go with it. These are the G chord and the A chord.

A chord

A

Chord studies

This song is a little faster, so we'll be using downstrums and upstrums.

The melody notes are on the high E, B, and G strings.

 53 & 54 **Example 20**

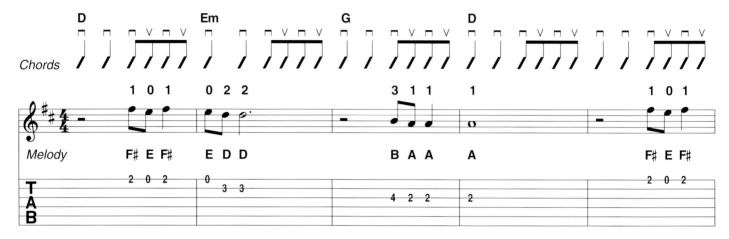

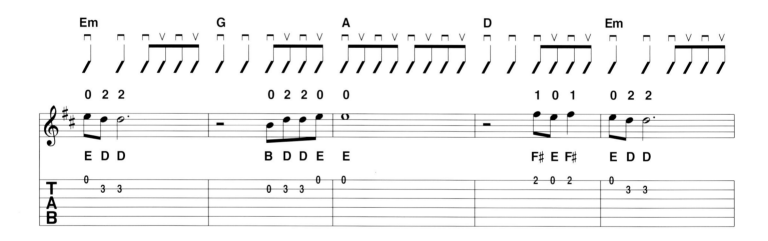

The melody of this next song has notes which
are found on the high E, B, G, D, and A strings.

 55 & 56 **Example 21**

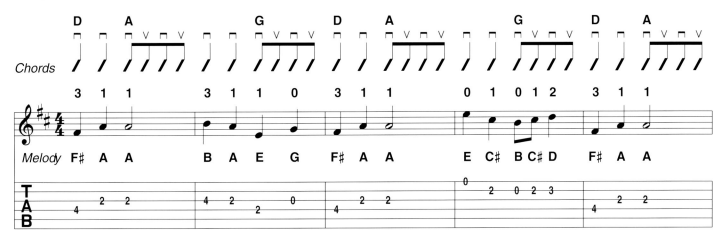

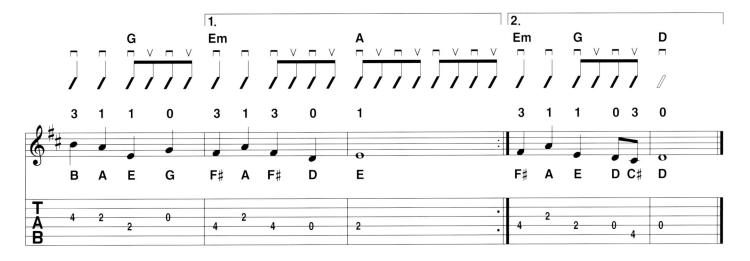

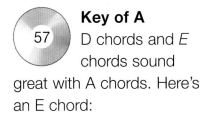 57 **Key of A**
D chords and *E*
chords sound
great with A chords. Here's
an E chord:

E chord

E

Chord studies

The notes for the melodies for these songs are
on the high E, B, and G strings.

58 & 59 Example 22

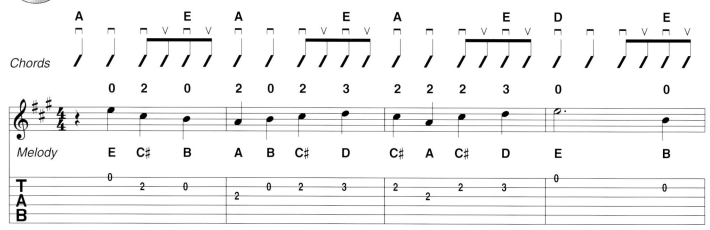

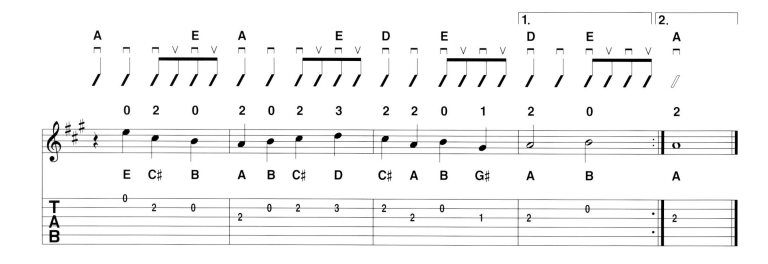

CHECKPOINT
WHAT YOU'VE ACHIEVED SO FAR

You can now:
- Play chords C, G, G7, Em, Am, F, D, A, and E (that's a lot!)
- Strum using upstrums and downstrums
- Play along to loads of cool tunes!

Keep going!

60 & 61 **Example 23**

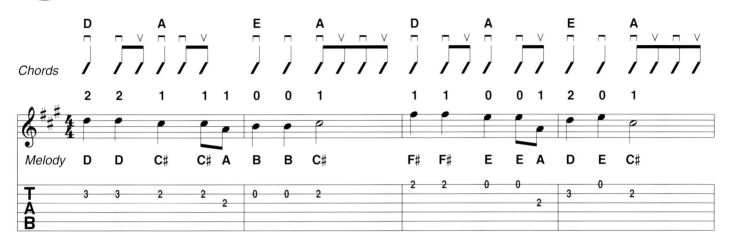

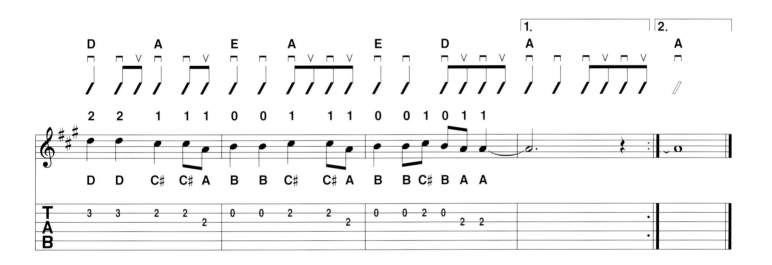

62

Key of E
E chords, A chords, and *B7* chords are often found together. The B7 chord is a little bit harder to play (you'll need *four* fingers for this one!) but with practice, you'll be doing it easily in no time.

B7 chord

B7

Chord studies

This next song is a little more difficult, so practise playing the E, A, and B7 chords until you can play them smoothly.

When you're ready, the notes for the melody are on the high E and B strings.

63 & 64 **Example 24**

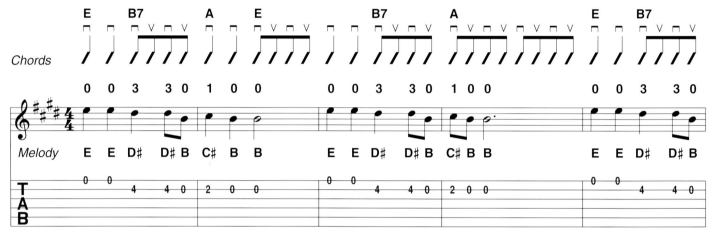

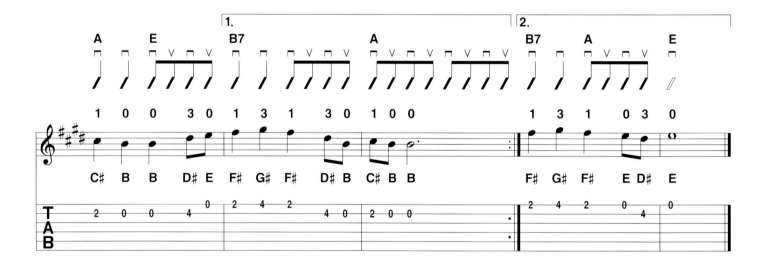

Other chords that sound good in E are *E7* and *A7*. They're very easy to play and here's what they look like:

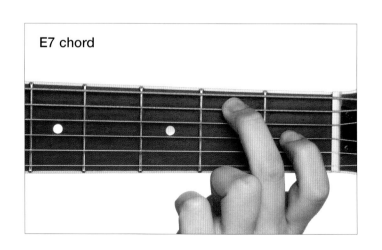

E7 chord

E7

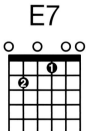

Now you're ready to play the blues. Pay extra attention to the melody... it's a little tricky!

A7 chord

A7

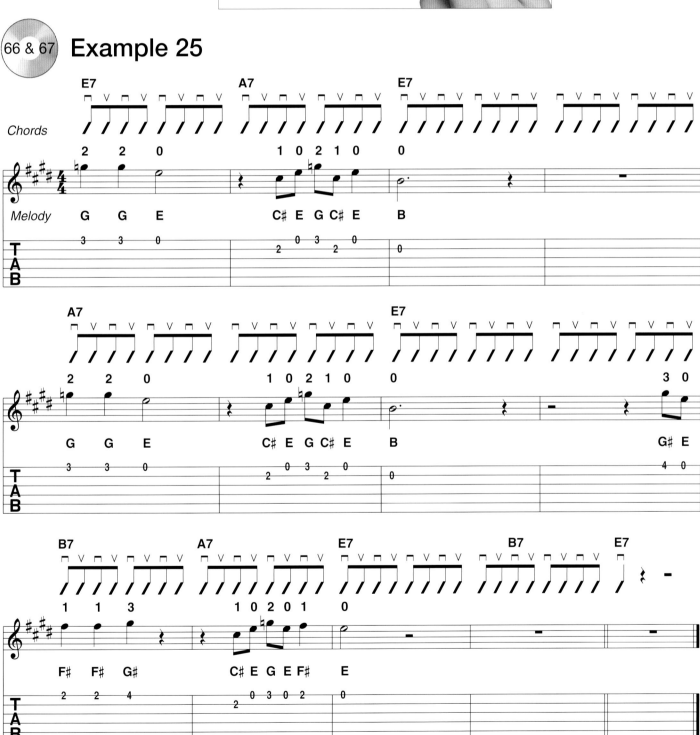

66 & 67 **Example 25**

More cool stuff to play

68

Congratulations... you've made it through all the lessons! Now you're ready for the fun stuff! The following songs are here for your practice and enjoyment. Each song has a melody line and chords.

If you have a teacher or a friend who plays guitar, you can learn and play one part while your teacher or friend plays the other. Or, you can learn both parts and then play along with the CD while a band backs you up. Have fun!

69–71 **Example 26**

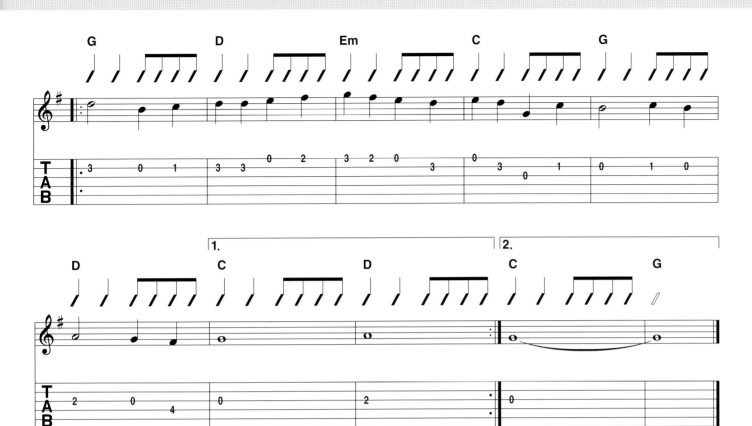

 **Example 27**

More cool stuff to play

78–80 **Example 29**

More cool stuff to play

Example 30

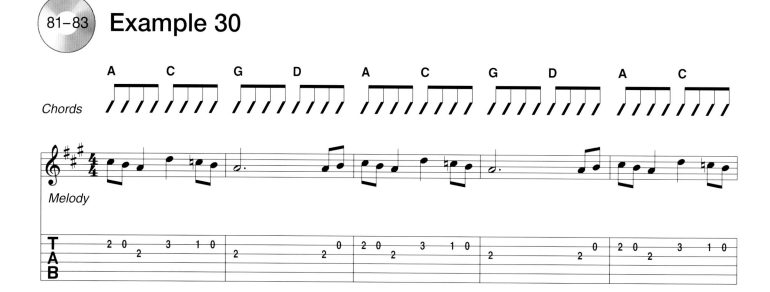

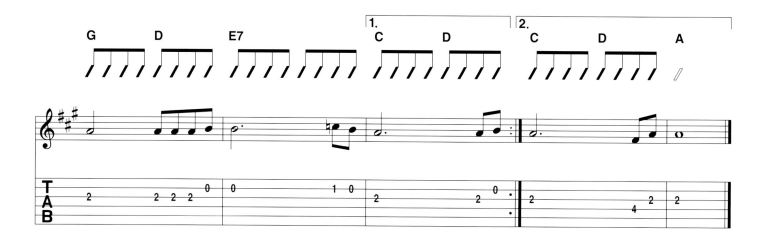

CHECKPOINT

Make sure…
…your guitar is in tune
…you are holding your guitar comfortably
…you are holding your pick correctly
…the strings are held down firmly – no buzzes!
…you are downstrumming ON the beat and upstrumming OFF
the beat, unless the song is at a slow speed.

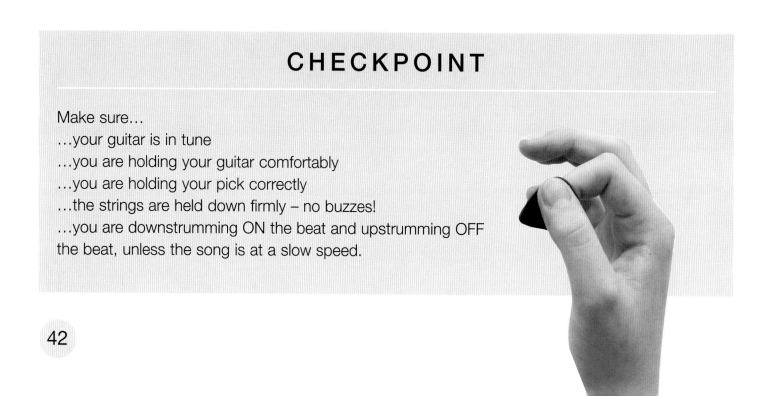

84-86 **Example 31**

Reading music and tablature

Music staff

The *music staff* contains the key signature, time signature, and notes. The *key signature* tells you what key you're in. For example, in the previous example, there are four sharp signs (♯) at the start of each staff. The first is on the F line; the second is on the C space; the third is on the G space; and the fourth is on the D line. This means that in this song, all Fs, Cs, Gs, and Ds are to be played as F♯, C♯, G♯ and D♯.

Time signature

The *time signature* contains two numbers, one on top of the other. The top number tells you how many beats are in a bar; the bottom number tells you what kind of note gets the beat. In our example, the time signature is $\frac{4}{4}$; therefore, there are four beats in a bar (because the top number is 4). The bottom 4 tells us that the quarter note gets the beat. If the time signature was $\frac{3}{8}$, then there would be three beats in a bar and the eighth note would get the beat.

Tablature

Tablature is a system of reading for guitar players. A *tablature staff* has six lines, each of which represents a string on a guitar. The highest tablature line represents the high E string; the line below represents the B string; the one below that represents the G string. The fourth tablature line represents the D string, and the fifth and sixth tablature lines are the A and E strings.

The *tab* numbers are the numbers of the frets that the notes are played on. In "Jingle Bells" above, the first note's tab number is a 2, which is shown to be on the B string. This means to play the note on the 2nd fret of the B string. A tab number of 0 means to play the open string (don't press on any frets).

Rhythms

o = Whole note. This kind of note gets 4 beats.

♩ = Half note. This note is half of a whole note; it gets 2 beats.

♩ = Quarter note. This note gets one beat.

♪ = Eighth note. This note gets half a beat.

To understand how these notes are related, see the following illustration.

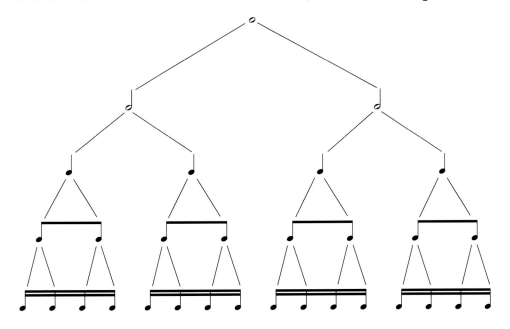

Rests

A rest is a period of silence in music. Just like notes, rests get a certain number of beats, depending on what kind of rest it is.

— = Whole rest. This kind of rest gets 4 beats.
In ⁴⁄₄, this would mean play nothing for a full bar.

— = Half rest. This rest is half of a whole rest; it gets 2 beats.

𝄽 = Quarter rest. This rest gets one beat.

𝄾 = Eighth rest. This rest gets half a beat.

Scale chart

The order of notes in a certain key is called a *scale*. practising scales is useful for getting used to where notes are on the fretboard. This makes learning to play songs you've never played before easier.

Below are the most common major scales. Remember, the numbers above the notes tell you which finger to play the notes with. Practise these slowly at first; as you get more comfortable with them, you'll be able to play them faster and faster.

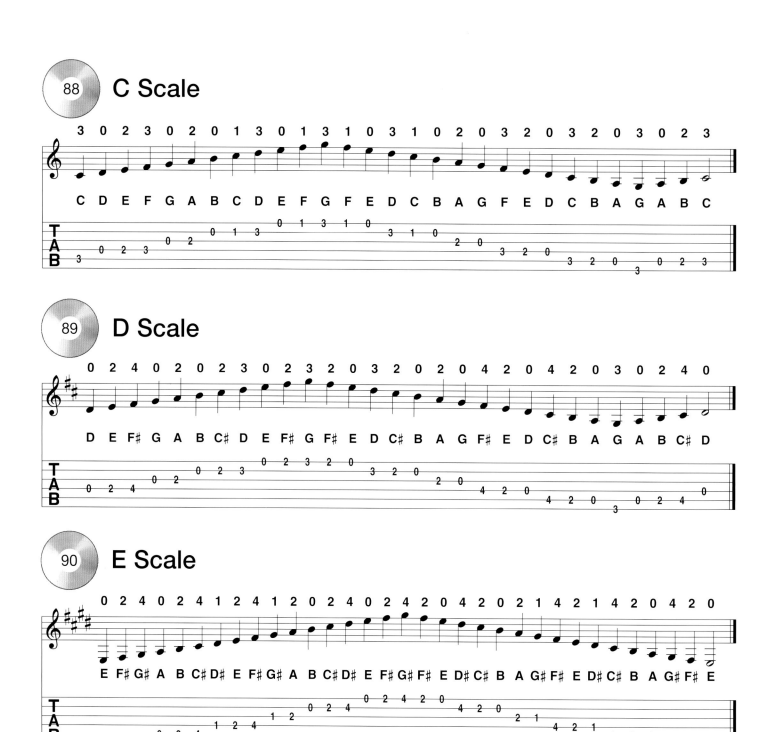

91 F Scale

92 G Scale

93 A Scale

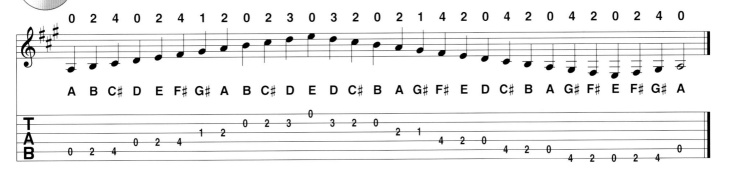

94 B Scale

Chord chart

Here is a chart with all the chords we've covered in this book.

A
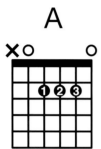

Am
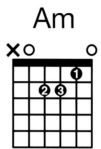

A7
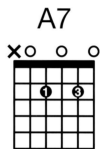

B7
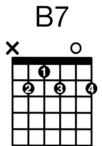

C
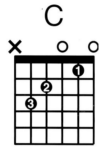

D
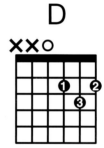

E
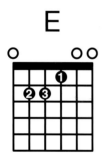

Em
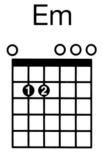

E7
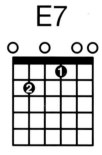

F
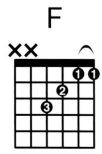

G
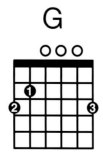

G7
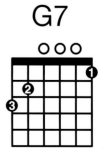

3/06(58449)